Contents

How to Use This Book

Reading serves as the major foundational skill for all school-based learning. The goal of *Reading Comprehension* is to increase learners' proficiency in reading comprehension skills at a third-grade level. The activities and skills in *Reading Comprehension* reflect national standards set by the International Reading Association (IRA). The subject matter involves curriculum-based fiction and nonfiction texts with a focus on grade-appropriate science and social studies topics.

Reading Comprehension features six sections that challenge learners to develop their literacy skills. Each section offers four curriculum-based activities with easy-to-follow directions as well as skill definitions and examples. The sections are: Parts of a Story, Understanding Text, Drawing from Text, Learning from Text, Different Forms of Writing, and Organizing Nonfiction.

Parts of a Story
The first section of this book focuses on the four components of a story: characters, setting, plot, and theme. After reading fictional texts, learners are asked to identify and answer questions about the different parts of a story.

Understanding Text
The second section of this book concentrates on learners' recognition of the main idea and supporting details of a story, as well as their abilities to compare and contrast information. After reading nonfiction passages, learners will answer questions and perform writing activities based on these concepts.

Drawing from Text
The third section of this book develops learners' abilities to determine cause and effect and to make inferences. The activities feature cause-and-effect clue words and sentences as well as questions requiring students to evaluate and draw logical conclusions based on nonfiction text.

Learning from Text
The fourth section of this book focuses on the location of facts in a story and the importance of following directions. Learners will identify answers to questions, follow clear directions, and follow a fun, healthy recipe as they strengthen their reading skills.

© Rosen School Supply•Brain Builders Reading Comprehension•3•RSS-8558-X

Different Forms of Writing

The fifth section of this book involves developing learners' abilities to recognize fiction and nonfiction text as well as their understanding of other forms of writing. Learners will read text, determine different types of writing based on the titles and features of a book, and learn how to write a simple poem about their feelings.

Organizing Nonfiction

The final section of this book concentrates on using a schedule, integrating knowledge using visualization skills, and determining the correct order of nonfiction events. Learners will answer questions based on a schedule, answer questions using a diagram related to text, and put events in chronological order.

Skills Correlation Guide

	Character and Plot	Setting and Theme	Main Idea	Supporting Details	Cause and Effect	Inferring Information	Comprehending Text	Following Directions	Understanding Different Types of Writing	Fiction and Nonfiction	Using Visuals to Draw Information	Putting Events in Order
Parts of a Story (pp. 11–15)	✓	✓					✓		✓	✓		
Understanding Text (pp. 17–21)			✓	✓						✓		
Drawing from Text (pp. 23–27)					✓	✓	✓					
Learning from Text (pp. 29–33)							✓	✓		✓		
Different Forms of Writing (pp. 35–39)							✓		✓	✓		
Organizing Nonfiction (pp. 41–45)										✓	✓	✓

The activities featured in this book are level N according to the guidelines set by Fountas and Pinnell.

© Rosen School Supply•Brain Builders Reading Comprehension•3•RSS-8558-X

Name _____

Character, Setting, Plot, and Theme

 Directions: Read the story and then answer the questions below.

Once upon a time, many happy mice lived in a house. One day, a cat moved into the house. The cat chased the mice around. The oldest mouse gathered all the mice together to come up with a plan to stop the cat. One mouse suggested that they tie a bell around the cat's neck while he was sleeping. That way, the mice would hear the bell when the cat was coming toward them. All of the mice liked this plan. However, not one of them was brave enough to climb onto the cat while he was sleeping. So the cat continued to chase them.

1. Who are the characters in this story? _____

2. Where does this story take place? _____

3. What is the theme of the story? _____

Name _____

Main Idea

 Directions: Read the paragraph and answer the questions below.

Fire safety is important. Knowing what to do if there is a fire can save your life. If there is a fire in your home, you must stay close to the ground and leave the building immediately. Do not stop to take anything with you. Never go back into a burning house. Go to a neighbor's house to call the police and fire department. If your clothes happen to catch on fire, remember to stop, drop to the ground, and roll around to put out the flames.

1. What is the main idea of this paragraph? _____

_____

2. What should you do if there is a fire in your home?

_____

_____

3. What should you do if your clothes catch on fire?

_____

_____

5

Name _____

Cause and Effect

 Directions: Read the sentences below. Circle the clue word that shows that each sentence is a cause-and-effect sentence.

1. Daniel and Justin were tired, so they decided to go to sleep.

2. Since we are sitting in the front row of the theater, we will be able to see the play well.

3. When the movie started, the lights were turned off.

4. Alison knew she would do well on her test because she had studied all week.

5. Since it is hot outside, we will go swimming today.

Name _____

Identifying Answers in Text

Directions: Read the paragraph and answer the questions below.

The aardvark is a hairy animal that lives in Africa. It has a long, narrow snout and a long, sticky tongue. The aardvark eats insects, such as ants and termites. It uses its claws to dig into the ground. Then it sticks out its tongue to grab the insects that live there. Aardvarks hunt at night and sleep during the day. They sleep in large holes that they dig in the ground.

1. Where does the aardvark live? _____

2. What does the aardvark eat? _____

3. When do aardvarks hunt? _____

4. Where do aardvarks sleep? _____

7

Name _____

Fiction and Nonfiction

 Directions: Read each paragraph below. Then decide whether it is fiction or nonfiction and circle your choice.

1. The beagle is a very friendly, playful dog. It has a lot of energy and enjoys running around. Beagles are small and muscular. Their fur is white, black, and tan. Beagles have floppy ears and brown eyes. They grow to be about 15 inches (38.1 centimeters) tall and can weigh up to 40 pounds (14.93 kilograms).

fiction   **nonfiction**

2. Mom and I went to an animal shelter today to find a dog. There were many types of dogs there. I really liked a puppy named Sam. A man who worked at the shelter told my mom that Sam was a beagle. My mom said that beagles were very friendly dogs. We decided that Sam should be the newest member of our family.

fiction   **nonfiction**

Name _____

Using Schedules

 Directions: Use Sara's summer camp schedule to answer the questions below.

8:30—breakfast	cafeteria	12:15—lunch	cafeteria
9:15—arts & crafts	building B, room 212	1:15—softball	field D
10:00—tennis	court 3	2:00—story time	building C, room 302
10:45—swim	pool 1	2:45—snack	cafeteria
11:30—music	building A, room 101	3:15—bus lineup	field A

1. How many times does Sara go to the cafeteria?

2. Where does Sara go for story time?

_____

3. What activity does Sara have on court 3?

_____

4. Where does Sara play softball?

9

Teaching Tips...

Background

- It is important for learners to comprehend the basic plots of fictional texts, determine what characters are featured in these texts, find the setting in which a story takes place, and determine the underlying theme an author wishes to convey to his or her audience.

Homework Helper

- Have a learner choose his or her favorite book. Guide that learner through the process of identifying the plot, characters, setting, and theme of that book. Working with a familiar text will help learners become more comfortable with the classification of the components of a story.

Research-based Activity

- It is important for learners to understand that there can be both fiction and nonfiction texts featuring the same subject. Provide learners with a fictional story about a topic, such as an animal or a historical figure, and ask them to find a nonfiction text in the library featuring that same topic. Have learners compare the two texts to gain a deeper understanding of the differences between fiction and nonfiction.

Test Prep

- The activities in this section require learners to recognize characteristics of a written passage. Development of this skill will help learners build the necessary foundation for success on classroom testing in this area.

Different Audiences

- Help a learner for whom English is a second language (ESL) master the skills in this section by using a story familiar to him or her. Using a familiar story that has been translated from the learner's native language can help that learner become more comfortable with the concepts of character, setting, plot, and theme.

Name _____

A Tale of Two Mice

The characters in a story are the people or animals that the story is about. The setting of a story is where and when the story takes place.

 Directions: Read the story and answer the questions below.

Once upon a time, there was a busy city mouse and a quiet country mouse. One day, the city mouse visited the country mouse. The country mouse welcomed her guest with a few crumbs of bread and a small piece of cheese. However, the city mouse was used to eating fancier food. She invited the country mouse home for dinner. The two mice went to the city mouse's home. There they found cookies, cake, and other tasty treats. Just as they began to eat, a cat ran into the room. The mice dropped their food and ran to hide. Later, as the country mouse was leaving to return to the country, she told the city mouse that she did not like the city.

1. Who are the characters in this story?

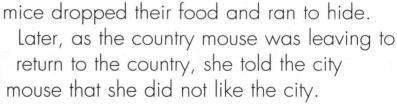

_____

_____

2. Is there more than one setting in this story? If

so, what are they? _____

_____

Name _____

The Grasshopper and the Ant

> The theme of a story is the message or idea of the story.

 Directions: Read the story and answer the questions below.

One day, a grasshopper sat in a field, enjoying the summer sunshine. He noticed an ant struggling to carry home a grain. The grasshopper laughed at the ant for working all day and not enjoying the beautiful weather. All summer long, the grasshopper sat in the sun, watching the ant slowly carry food to his house. When the weather turned cold, it began to snow. The grasshopper looked for food but could not find any. The ant had saved lots of food. The grasshopper begged the ant for food, but the ant needed what he had saved for himself. The grasshopper was left hungry and sad.

1. What did the grasshopper do all summer long? _____

_____

2. How did the ant prepare for winter? _____

_____

3. What is the theme of this story? _____

_____

 **The story above is called a fable. Find another fable in your library.**

© Rosen School Supply•Brain Builders Reading Comprehension•3•RSS-8558-X

Name _____

The Lion and the Mouse

> The characters in a story are the people or animals that the story is about. The plot of a story is what the story is about. The theme of a story is the message of the story.

 Directions: Read the story and answer the questions below. Use a separate sheet of paper if you need more space.

One afternoon, a mouse passed by a sleeping lion. The mouse squeaked and woke the lion. The angry lion decided to eat the mouse. The mouse begged the lion to spare him. He promised that if the lion let him live, he would one day repay the lion for his kindness. The lion laughed, wondering how a mouse might help a lion, but he let the mouse go. A little while later, the mouse heard a terrible noise from where the lion was sleeping. The mouse found the lion caught in a rope trap. The mouse chewed through the ropes and freed the lion. From then on, they were best friends.

1. Who are the characters in this story? _____

2. What is the plot of this story? _____

_____

3. What is the theme of this story? _____

13

Name _____

A Woodcutter's Wishes

The plot of a story is what happens to the characters in the story.

 Directions: Read the story and answer the questions below. Use a separate sheet of paper if you need more space.

A woodcutter went into the forest to cut down a large oak tree. Just as he was about to cut down the tree a fairy appeared. She said that if he spared the tree she would grant him three wishes. The woodcutter agreed and rushed home to his wife. His wife warned her husband not to waste his wishes. Later, the hungry woodcutter wished for an apple. When an apple appeared his wife yelled at him. The woodcutter didn't like his wife's yelling and he wished she had an apple on her nose. Then, an apple appeared on his wife's nose. The man pulled on it, but the apple was stuck. He then had to use his third wish to remove the apple.

1. What was the woodcutter going to do in the woods? _____

2. What did the fairy promise the woodcutter if he spared the oak tree?

_____

3. What was the woodcutter's first wish? _____

4. What happened to the woodcutter's wife? _____

Write a paragraph explaining the plot of your favorite book.

14

Name _____

Skill Check—Parts of a Story

Character, Setting, and Theme

 Directions: Read the story and then answer the questions below. Use a separate sheet of paper if you need more space.

Once there was a farmer who had many sons who fought all the time. They hated to work together on the farm. One day, the farmer brought out a bundle of sticks and gave each son a chance to break the bundle in half. Each son failed to break the bundle. The father then unwrapped the bundle and handed each son a stick. Each son was able to break his stick easily. The father explained to the sons that by working together they were strong like the bundle of sticks.

1. Who are the characters of this story? _____

_____

2. Where does this story take place?

_____

3. What is the theme of

this story? _____

_____

15

Teaching Tips...

Background

- Learners at this level should be comfortable identifying the main idea and supporting details of a story, as well as using these features to compare and contrast the information given in two different texts.

Homework Helper

- Help learners focus on the details of a story by having them create a shoe-box diorama of a chosen scene from a story. Have learners write an explanatory paragraph featuring the details of that scene to accompany the diorama.

Research-based Activity

- Have each learner choose a book from the library. Have the learners read their books and write a short paragraph explaining the main idea of the book and the details that support that idea.

Test Prep

- The activities in this section require learners to read passages of text and answer questions based on those passages. Learners will be tested on their ability to locate information in a given passage on standardized tests through elementary and higher grades.

Different Audiences

- Help a challenged learner master the identification of the main idea and supporting details of a story by having him or her fill out a blank story web. A story web is a visual tool that features labeled circles. Draw and label a main idea circle in the center of a page. Draw and label several detail circles that branch out from the main idea circle. Have the challenged learner use the diagram to organize the main idea and details of a story.

16

Snail Shells

The main idea is the general meaning of a paragraph. We find the main idea by reading the sentences that make up the paragraph.

 Directions: Read the paragraph about snail shells and answer the questions below. Use a separate sheet of paper if you need more room.

All snails have shells that cover their bodies. Snail shells can be different colors, shapes, and sizes. A snail's shell is very strong. It protects the snail's body from drying out. A snail's shell also protects the snail from animals that might eat them.

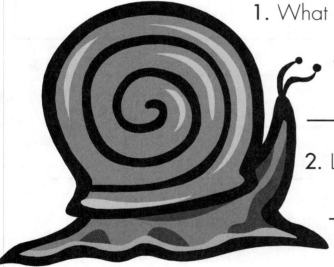

1. What is the main idea of the paragraph

   above? _____

   _____

2. List one way snail shells protect snails.

   _____

3. List another way snail shells

protect snails. _____

 **Choose a paragraph from your favorite book. Write down the main idea of that paragraph.**

17

Name _____

Electrical Storms

The main idea is the general meaning of a paragraph. We find the main idea by reading the sentences that make up the paragraph.

 Directions: Read the paragraph and answer the questions below.

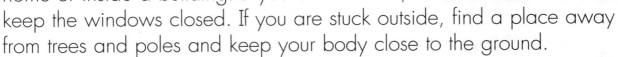

An electrical storm is a storm with thunder and lightning. These storms can be dangerous. There are several ways you can stay safe during an electrical storm. You are safest at home or inside a building. If you are in a car, keep the windows closed. If you are stuck outside, find a place away from trees and poles and keep your body close to the ground.

1. What is the main idea of this paragraph? _____

_____

2. What is an electrical storm? _____

3. What are the two safest places to be during an electrical storm?

_____

4. What should you do if you are in a car during an electrical storm?

_____

 **Write a paragraph about your own experience watching a lightning storm.**

Name _____

Dalmatians and Pugs

When you compare and contrast things, you are judging the similarities and differences between them. Organizing information can help you to compare and contrast.

 Directions: Read the paragraph. Then fill in the chart by writing the information where it belongs.

Dogs can be many sizes and colors. The dalmatian is a large dog. It has a white coat with black spots. Dalmatians are very active dogs. They need a lot of exercise. Another type of dog is the pug. It is a small dog. The pug's coat can be tan or black. Pugs are not very active dogs. They do not need much exercise.

	Dalmatian	**Pug**
Size		
Color		
Exercise		

Name _____

Mako and Lemon Sharks

When you compare and contrast things, you are judging the similarities and differences between them. Organizing information can help you to compare and contrast.

 Directions: Read the paragraphs below about two different sharks. On a separate sheet of paper, write your own paragraph comparing and contrasting the sharks.

The mako shark is a large shark. It can grow to be 12 feet (3.7 meters) long. Mako sharks live in areas of the Atlantic and Pacific oceans that have cool waters. Mako sharks are very fast swimmers. Mako sharks have been known to attack people.

   The lemon shark is named for the yellow color of its back. Lemon sharks usually grow to be about 10 feet (3.1 m) long. The lemon shark is often found in the warm waters of the Pacific Ocean, off the coasts of Central and South America. Lemon sharks have attacked people swimming in their territory.

 **Read about at least three more kinds of sharks on the Internet or in an encyclopedia.**

20

Name _____

Skill Check—Understanding Text

Main Idea

 Directions: Read the paragraph. On a separate sheet of paper, answer the questions below.

There are different types of environments on Earth. Each of these environments has different temperatures, different amounts of moisture, and different plant and animal life. These environments are called biomes. Some examples of biomes are deserts, tundras, forests, and grasslands.

1. What is the main idea of this paragraph?

2. What are three types of biomes?

Compare and Contrast

 Directions: Read the paragraphs. On a separate sheet of paper, write your own paragraph comparing and contrasting the two kinds of dinosaurs.

The supersaurus was one of the longest dinosaurs ever discovered. It was close to 138 feet (42.1 m) long and 54 feet (16.5 m) tall. It was a herbivore, eating only plants. The supersaurus lived during the Jurassic Period.

The iguanodon was a dinosaur that lived during the Cretaceous Period. The iguanodon was about 30 feet (9.1 m) long and close to 16 feet (4.9 m) tall. It was a herbivore, eating only plants to survive.

Teaching Tips...

For *Drawing from Text* (pp. 23–27)

Background

• In this section, learners will identify cause-and-effect clue words, determine the cause and the effect in various sentences, and make inferences after reading passages. Becoming comfortable with the concepts of cause and effect will prepare learners to write cause-and-effect essays later in their academic careers. Making inferences based on reading texts enables learners to develop their logical reasoning abilities.

Homework Helper

• After completing the Cause-and-Effect Clue Words activity on page 23, have learners write their own cause-and-effect sentences using the featured clue words.

Research-based Activity

• After completing the Beluga Whales activity on page 25, have learners research another whale of their choice on the Internet. Ask learners to write a paragraph about what they have learned and read it to you. Ask the learners questions, prompting them to make inferences based on what they have learned.

Test Prep

• As learners develop their logical reasoning abilities, they become better test takers. This essential skill is tested through various subjects at this level.

Different Audiences

• Have accelerated learners write a cause-and-effect paragraph that explains why or how something happened. Provide them with a topic and the necessary information.

22

Name _____

Cause-and-Effect Clue Words

A cause is the reason for an event or action. An effect is what happens as a result of a cause. Cause-and-effect sentences often use clue words such as because, so, when, and since to show the relationship between two actions.

Example: Ella threw out the apple (because) it was rotten.

 Directions: Read the sentences below. Circle the clue word that shows that each sentence is a cause-and-effect sentence.

1. The class trip was called off because it began to snow.

2. When the speaker began to talk, the audience became quiet.

3. She was not feeling well, so her mother let her stay home from school.

4. Since my brother came home late, we ate dinner later than usual.

 **Write three cause-and-effect sentences using the clue words listed above.**

Name _____

Cause-and-Effect Sentences

A cause is the reason for an event or action. An effect is what happens as a result of a cause.

Example: <u>The car stopped quickly</u> because a squirrel ran across the road.

 Directions: Circle the cause and underline the effect in each sentence below. They can appear in any order.

1. We needed milk, so we went to the store to buy some.

2. My father took me to the doctor because I was not feeling well.

3. Since I got up early this morning, I am tired.

4. The game was cancelled because of the storm.

 5. Since I finished my homework, I am allowed to watch television.

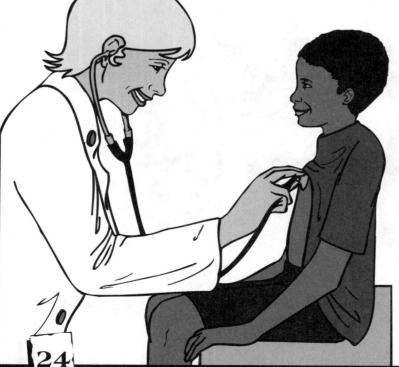

 Listen to your family speaking. See if you can pick out cause-and-effect sentences when they have a conversation.

24

Name _____

Beluga Whales

Sometimes we must draw a conclusion that is not directly stated in the text we read.

 Directions: Read the paragraph and answer the questions below.

The beluga whale is a type of white whale. Beluga whales can grow to be 15 feet (4.6 meters) long, which is smaller than most whales. Unlike most whales, beluga whales can turn their heads from side to side. Beluga whales swim in the icy waters of the Arctic Circle.

1. Do you think most whales are lighter or darker than Beluga whales?

_____

2. Do most whales grow to be bigger or smaller than 15 feet long?

_____

3. Can most whales turn their heads from side to side? _____

4. Do beluga whales like warm or cold waters? _____

 **Find out if there are beluga whales at an aquarium near you and see them for yourself.**

Name _____

Gorillas

Sometimes we must draw a conclusion that is not directly stated in the text we read.

 Directions: Read the paragraph and answer the questions below.

Gorillas are part of a group of animals called primates that also includes monkeys and humans. The different types of gorillas are mountain gorillas, eastern lowland, and western lowland gorillas. Gorillas live in rain forests throughout different parts of central Africa. Gorillas take care of one another and spend a lot of time with their families.

1. How do you think the mountain gorilla got its

   name? _____

   _____

2. How many types of gorillas are there?

   _____

3. Other than gorillas, what else belong to the

primate group? _____

4. Gorillas enjoy living in groups. Why?_____

26 _____

Name _____

Skill Check—Drawing from Text

Cause and Effect

 Directions: Read the sentences below. Circle the clue word that shows that each sentence is a cause-and-effect sentence.

1. The boy felt proud because he did well on his science test.

2. Since we could not go to the park, my father took us to the movies.

Making Inferences

 Directions: Read the paragraph. On a separate sheet of paper, answer the questions below.

When you speak, the air you breathe passes through a part of your body called your voice box. The air traveling in and out of your throat makes your vocal cords and voice box move. This helps to form the sounds that come out of your mouth.

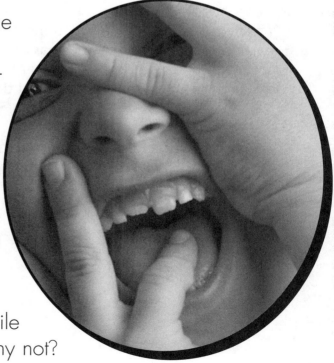

1. What do you think would happen to your voice if you increased the amount of air used to speak?

2. Do you think you could speak while holding your breathe? Why or why not?

27

Background

• Identifying answers in text and following directions are skills essential for success in all classroom studies. National standards recommend learners master these skills as early as possible. The activities in this section strengthen learners' abilities in these areas.

Homework Helper

• After completing the Reading a Recipe activity on page 32, have learners find a recipe in a cookbook or on the Internet. Then ask the learner questions about it after he or she has read their recipe.

Research-based Activity

• Have learners use a map to write down directions from their homes to a familiar place, such as the school or a store. As learners create directions, they will gain insight into the importance of clear, concise directions.

Test Prep

• Proficiency in following directions is an indispensable tool in test taking. Learners should practice and master this skill early in their academic careers. In addition, learners benefit from practicing identifying answers in text as this skill is frequently tested through standardized testing.

Different Audiences

• Challenge an accelerated learner by having him or her read a newspaper or magazine article. Ask the learner questions, prompting him or her to identify the answers in the article.

TEACHING TIPS

Name _____

Earthworms

By reading a paragraph, we can answer questions to find the information we need.

 Directions: Read the paragraph and answer the questions below.

An earthworm is a worm that lives in the dirt. Most earthworms are brown. Earthworm bodies are made up of many sections called segments. Earthworms have five hearts that work together to carry blood through their bodies. Some earthworms are very small. Others can grow to be several feet long.

1. What color are most earthworms? _____

2. What are earthworms bodies made up of? _____

3. How many hearts do earthworms have? _____

4. Where do earthworms live? _____

 **Find out about another kind of worm by doing research in the library.**

Name _____

Turtles

We can answer questions by reading a paragraph to find the information we need.

 Directions: Read the paragraph and answer the questions below.

Turtles are an ancient group of animals. There were turtles on Earth more than 200 million years ago. Today there are more than 55 kinds of turtles that live in the United States and Canada. The most common turtle in the United States is the painted turtle. These turtles are often found near ponds.

1. How long have turtles lived on

Earth? _____

_____

2. How many kinds of turtles are there in the United States and

Canada? _____

3. What is the most common turtle in the United States? _____

4. Where are painted turtles often found? _____

 Find out the differences between a turtle and a tortoise by doing research on the Internet.

Name _____

Follow Along!

Directions are instructions about what to do, how to do something, where to go, or how to get to a place. It is important to learn to follow directions.

 Directions: Read each direction and do what it says to do.

1. Circle all of the words below that name a day of the week.
2. Underline each word that names a vegetable.
3. Draw a line between the two words that make up each compound word.
4. Draw a box around the word with the most syllables.

cucumber	Tuesday	bookmark
Thursday	Saturday	carrot
dictionary	basketball	potato
keyboard	Monday	summertime

 **Ask an adult to help you write down directions from your house to your school.**

Name _____

Reading a Recipe

A recipe is a set of directions we follow to cook food. We follow the directions in the order they are listed.

 Directions: Read the recipe and answer the questions below.

Cinnamon Apple Smoothie

- Wash and peel an apple.
- Cut up the apple and throw away the seeds.
- Place apple pieces into a blender.
- Add 1 cup of milk.
- Add 1 cup of vanilla yogurt.
- Add 1/2 teaspoon of cinnamon.
- Add 6 ice cubes and blend.

1. What goes into the blender first ? _____

2. How many teaspoons of cinnamon should you use to make the

   smoothie? _____

3. What is the fourth direction in the recipe? _____

4. How many ice cubes does the recipe ask for? _____

Name _____

Skill Check—Learning from Text

Identifying Answers in Text

 Directions: Read the paragraph and answer the questions below.

Ospreys are large brown-and-white birds. They are related to hawks and eagles. Ospreys can be found on every continent except for Antarctica. Ospreys eat fish. An osprey dives into the water to catch a fish. It then rises out of the water and carries the fish to land to eat.

1. What two birds are ospreys related to? _____

2. How do ospreys catch fish? _____

Following Directions

 Directions: Read and follow each direction below.

1. Circle the words that name fruits.

2. Underline the words that name months.

3. Draw a line between the words that make up a compound word.

peach   January   March   haircut   banana

Background

• As learners develop an understanding of what separates fiction and non-fiction writing, they develop a deeper understanding of what is real and make believe in the world around them. In addition, it is important for learners to develop a basic awareness of different forms of writing at an early age. This awareness will better prepare learners to do research papers in higher grades.

Homework Helper

• After completing the Poetry activity on page 38, have learners write a similar poem about an experience in which they did not feel happy. This exercise can help learners become more comfortable sharing their feelings in writing.

Research-based Activity

• Assign each learner a person of historical significance. Have learners use three different forms of writing, such as encyclopedias, biographies, auto-biographies, etc., to learn about that person.

Test Prep

• The activities in this section provide learners with practice in advancing their knowledge of different forms of writing. This practice is necessary for success in language arts classroom testing. National standards recommend that learners be able to read, respond to, and distinguish between different forms of literature at this level.

Different Audiences

• Help a challenged learner understand the difference between fiction and nonfiction by providing them with examples of each type of writing about one subject. For example, offer the learner a nonfiction account of a sports figure's life as well as a fictional story about a day in that person's life.

Name _____

Feelings

Fiction stories are about imaginary people, places, and events. Nonfiction stories are about real people, places, and events.

 Directions: Read each paragraph below. Then circle whether it is fiction or nonfiction.

1. Anna had a bad day at school today. She did not do well on her math test. Then she had a fight with her friend. After school, Anna told her mother how sad she felt. Anna's mother explained that everyone has bad days once in a while. Anna smiled, knowing that tomorrow would be a better day.

fiction   nonfiction

2. Talking about your feelings is important. Sharing how you feel with someone you trust can help you learn to understand why you feel a certain way. It can even help you feel better when you feel sad. Sharing your feelings can also help you feel closer to the people who care about you.

fiction   nonfiction

 **Write down three feelings you had today. Think of what you were doing when you felt each way.**

© Rosen School Supply•Brain Builders Reading Comprehension•3•RSS-8558-X

Name _____

Book Titles

Fiction stories are about imaginary people, places, and events.
Nonfiction stories are about real people, places, and events.

 Directions: Read each book title below. Then decide whether it is the title of a fiction or a nonfiction book. Write your answer on the line provided.

1. *The Student's Dictionary* _____

2. *A Dog Named Sally* _____

3. *The Adventures of Super Sam* _____

4. *The Cool Cookbook for Kids* _____

5. *Tori Learns to Read* _____

6. *Animals of the Rain Forest* _____

 Write down the title of your favorite book. Is the book fiction or nonfiction?

Name _____

The Right Book

Fiction stories are about imaginary people, places, and things. Encyclopedias are books that list information about real people, places, and things. Atlases are books with maps and information about different places.

 Directions: Decide which book you would look in to find out about the information listed below. Write F if you would look in a *fiction* book, write E if you would look in an *encyclopedia*, or write A if you would look in an *atlas*. There might be more than one answer for each question.

1. the inventions of Benjamin Franklin _____

2. a map of Australia _____

3. what happened in chapter 3 _____

4. the types of food alligators eat _____

5. whether or not there are mountains in South America _____

 **Use an atlas to find a map of China.**

Name _____

Poetry

Poetry is writing that expresses the writer's imagination. In a poem, the sounds of the patterns of the words often have special importance. Some poems rhyme, but others do not.

 Directions: Think of somewhere that makes you feel happy, such as a place you have visited. Complete the following sentences to create a poem about that place.

I see _____

I hear _____

I smell _____

I taste _____

I feel _____

I think _____

38

Name _____

Skill Check—Different Forms of Writing

Fiction and Nonfiction

 Directions: Read the paragraph below. Then circle whether it is fiction or nonfiction.

Medicine is used to make you feel better when you are sick. Some medicines are pills and others are liquids that you drink. Medicines can be made from natural plants. Medicines can also be made and tested by scientists in laboratories.

fiction   nonfiction

Types of Writing

 Directions: Decide which book you would look in to find out about the information listed below. Write F if you would look in a *fiction* book, write E if you would look in an *encyclopedia*, or write A if you would look in an *atlas*.

1. what happened to the main character in chapter 5 _____

2. where George Washington was born _____

Teaching Tips...

TEACHING TIPS

Background

• Using schedules, relating visual representations to text, and organizing text chronologically are skills introduced in the classroom at this level. The following activities offer curriculum-correlated practice on these topics.

Homework Helper

• Have learners write out their weekly schedules, including meals eaten with their families, hours spent at school, after-school activities, bedtimes, etc.

Research-based Activity

• After completing the Abraham Lincoln activity on page 43, have learners find out more about Lincoln's life by doing research on the Internet. Ask learners to write a paragraph about what they have learned.

Test Prep

• The activities in this section provide learners with the opportunity to build a strong foundation in organizing nonfiction. Practicing the skills covered in the following activities will help learners succeed on language arts classroom tests.

Different Audiences

• Visual representations of text, used in tandem with text, can help learners for whom English is a second language (ESL) understand texts more clearly. Provide these learners with diagrams, charts, maps, and illustrations related to nonfiction texts. The visual aids will help the learners understand any unfamiliar language.

Name _____

Ryan's Schedule

We use schedules to keep track of when to do certain things, such as going to a class.

 Directions: Use the schedule to answer the questions below.

8:45—math	room 320	*12:15*—lunch	cafeteria
9:55—language arts	room 246	*1:05*—science	room 131
11:15—social studies	room 301	*1:55*—art	room 206

1. What room does Ryan go to for his art class? _____

2. What class is Ryan in at 11:15? _____

3. What class does Ryan have in room 131?

 **Write down three types of schedules you have used before.**

Name _____

Our Solar System

 Directions: Read the paragraph and look at the diagram of our solar system. Then answer the questions.

Our solar system is made up of nine planets and the Sun. The nine planets move around the Sun. The planets closest to the Sun are Mercury, Venus, Earth, and Mars. They are made up mostly of rock and have very few moons. The planets farthest from the Sun are Jupiter, Saturn, Uranus, Neptune, and Pluto. They are made up mostly of gases and have many moons.

1. Which planet is farthest from the Sun? _____

2. Which planets have very few moons? _____

_____

_____

3. Which planets are made

mostly of gases? _____

_____

_____

_____

_____

42

Name _____

Abraham Lincoln

It is important to recognize the proper order of events in a story.

 Directions: Read the story. Number the sentences at the bottom of the page from 1 to 5 to show the correct order of the story.

Abraham Lincoln was born in 1809. He lived in a log cabin as a young boy. In 1836, Lincoln became a lawyer. Several years later he married Mary Todd. They had four children together. Lincoln became the sixteenth president of the United States in 1861.

_____ Abraham Lincoln and Mary Todd get married.

_____ Abraham Lincoln lives in a log cabin.

_____ Abraham Lincoln and Mary Todd have four children.

_____ Abraham Lincoln becomes the

president of the United States.

_____ Abraham Lincoln is born.

 **Find out who were the presidents immediately before and after Abraham Lincoln.**

Name _____

George Washington

It is important to recognize the proper order of events in a story.

 Directions: Number the sentences from 1 to 4 to show the correct order of the story.

_____ George married Martha Custis in 1759.

_____ George Washington was born in 1732.

_____ George became the first president

of the United States in 1789.

_____ George spent his early childhood

years in Fredericksburg, Virginia.

 Look up George Washington in an encyclopedia and write three more sentences about his life to add to this story. Remember to keep them in the proper order.

Name _____

Skill Check—Organizing Nonfiction

Using Schedules

 Directions: Use Carly's after-school schedule to answer the questions below.

Monday	4:30	ballet	Thursday	3:00		soccer
Tuesday	3:45	gymnastics	Friday	2:20		painting

1. Where does Carly go on

Thursday at 3:00? _____

2. When does Carly have ballet?

_____

Order of Events

 Directions: Number the sentences from 1 to 3 to show the correct order of the story.

_____ Benjamin Franklin signed the Declaration of Independence in 1776.

_____ Benjamin Franklin was born on January 17, 1706.

_____ From 1733 to 1758, Benjamin Franklin wrote a yearly book with useful information including a calendar and weather information called *Poor Richard's Almanac*.

45

Answer Key

p. 4
1. mice, cat
2. in a house
3. If you are always afraid to try, you'll never succeed.

p. 5
1. how to stay safe if there is a fire in your house
2. stay close to the ground and leave the building immediately
3. stop, drop, and roll

p. 6
1. *so* is circled
2. *since* is circled
3. *when* is circled
4. *because* is circled
5. *since* is circled

p. 7
1. in Africa
2. insects, such as ants and termites
3. at night
4. in large holes

p. 8
1. nonfiction
2. fiction

p. 9
1. 3
2. building C, room 302
3. tennis
4. field D

p. 11
1. the city mouse, the country mouse, and the cat
2. yes; first the country and then the city

p. 12
1. sat in the sun enjoying the beautiful weather
2. He carried food to his house every day to store for the winter.
3. It is important to work hard and to be prepared.

p. 13
1. a lion and a mouse
2. A lion spares a mouse's life and the mouse returns the favor by saving the lion's life.
3. If you help others, they will help you.

p. 14
1. cut down an oak tree
2. that she would grant his next three wishes

3. that he had an apple
4. She had an apple stuck to her nose.

p. 15
1. a farmer and his sons
2. on a farm
3. A group of people working together is stronger than a single person doing the same job.

p. 17
1. Snails have shells that cover their bodies.
2. Answers will vary but should reflect the information stated in the text.
3. Answers will vary but should reflect the information stated in the text.

p. 18
1. how to stay safe during an electrical storm
2. a storm with thunder and lightning
3. at home or inside a building
4. keep the windows closed

p. 19
Size: Dalmatians are large; pugs are small.

Color: Dalmatians have white coats with black spots; pugs have tan or black coats.

Exercise: Dalmatians need a lot of exercise; pugs do not.

p. 20
Answers will vary but should reflect the information stated in the text.

p. 21
Main Idea
1. There are different types of environments on Earth.
2. Answers will vary but should reflect the information stated in the text.

Compare and Contrast
Answers will vary but should reflect the information stated in the text.

p. 23
1. *because* is circled
2. *When* is circled
3. *so* is circled
4. *Since* is circled

p. 24
1. cause: We needed milk; effect: so we went to the store to buy some
2. cause: I was not feeling well; effect: My father took me to the doctor
3. cause: I got up early this morning: effect: I am tired
4. cause: the storm; effect: The game was cancelled
5. cause: I finished my homework; effect: I am allowed to watch television

p. 25
1. darker
2. bigger
3. no
4. cold

p. 26
1. it lives in the mountains
2. three
3. monkeys and humans
4. because they take care of each other and spend time with their families

p. 27
Cause and Effect
1. *because* is circled
2. *Since* is circled

Making Inferences
1. it would become louder
2. no, you need air to move your vocal chords and voice box

p. 29
1. brown
2. sections called segments
3. five
4. in the dirt

p. 30
1. for more than 200 million years
2. more than 55
3. the painted turtle
4. near ponds

p. 31
cucumber (Tuesday) bookmark
(Thursday) (Saturday) carrot
dictionary basketball potato
keyboard (Monday) summertime

p. 32
1. apple pieces
2. 1/2 teaspoon
3. add 1 cup of milk
4. 6

p. 33
Identifying Answers in Text
1. hawks and eagles
2. by diving into the water

47

Following Directions

(peach)　January　March

haircut　(banana)

p. 35
1. fiction
2. nonfiction

p. 36
1. nonfiction
2. fiction
3. fiction
4. nonfiction
5. fiction
6. nonfiction

p. 37
1. E
2. A
3. F
4. E
5. A or E

p. 38
Answers will vary.

p. 39
Fiction and Nonfiction
nonfiction

Types of Writing
1. F
2. E

p. 41
1. 206
2. social studies
3. science

p. 42
1. Pluto
2. the planets closest to the Sun: Mercury, Venus, Earth, and Mars
3. the outer planets, Jupiter, Saturn, Uranus, Neptune, and Pluto

p. 43
3　Abraham Lincoln and Mary Todd get married.

2　Abraham Lincoln lives in a log cabin.

4　Abraham Lincoln and Mary Todd have four children.

5　Abraham Lincoln becomes the president of the United States.

1　Abraham Lincoln is born.

p. 44
3　George married Martha Custis in 1759.

1　George Washington was born in 1732.

4　George became the first president of the United States in 1789.

2　George spent his early childhood years in Fredericksburg, Virginia.

p. 45
Using Schedules
1. soccer
2. Monday at 4:30

Order of Events
3　Benjamin Franklin signed the Declaration of Independence in 1776.

1　Benjamin Franklin was born on January 17,1706.

2　From 1733 to 1758, Benjamin Franklin wrote a yearly book with useful information including a calendar and weather information called *Poor Richard's Almanac*.

© Rosen School Supply•Brain Builders Reading Comprehension•3•RSS-8558-X

Eken Press Limited
87 Fore Street, Hertford,
Hertfordshire, SG14 1AL UK

Feng Shui Flow – Create Sustainable Interiors
© 2021 Susanna Utbult, Jenny Jonsson and Stevali fakta

First edition
ISBN 978-1-908233-33-2

English Translation: Ric Morris and Susanna Utbult
Photos: Maria Lacik, Jenny Jonsson, Susanna Utbult
Graphic Design: Jessica V Nyström & Alan Maranik

Printing: Print Best, Estonia 2021

Feng Shui Flow

Create Sustainable Interiors

Susanna Utbult
& Jenny Jonsson

EKEN
PRESS

Content

5

Foreword by Simon Brown

Feng Shui Flow

Feng shui means *wind water* and the name suggests it explores the movement of wind and water through nature, humans and homes. We know that about 70% of a human is simply a flow of water and that the particles in this water may have previously flowed through rivers, lakes and seas. Further, the same particles may have flowed through plants, insects, fish, animals and other humans. Water flows through nature connecting us to every other entity.

At the same time we are breathing, and through this we enjoy a connection to everything green on our planet. Vegetation creates oxygen and we need the oxygen that the wind brings us for life.

In this sense, feng shui is the exploration of how humans are connected to their environment. Further, we try to appreciate and understand the ebb and flow these connections create within each person. How do the weather, time of day, lunar cycle and seasons influence our emotions and moods? Do we feel or even think differently living by the sea, on the side of a mountain, in farm lands or in a city? Is it possible that our life might unfold differently living at the top of an urban high rise, compared to a cottage in a forest?

When considering the interior of a home, we might consider how a combination of wind and water, in the form of steam, might flow through each room. This would represent the flow of chi.

Chi, literally meaning vital breath, can be seen as the flow of all things between the polarity of yin-yang. The change of atmosphere from night to day is described by the flow of chi, from yin to yang. Just as the flow of bright yang sunshine chi coming in from a southern window will flow to the darker more yin corners at the back of a room. These currents of chi help us choose where to sit, sleep, work, relax so that we immerse ourselves in the ideal flow of chi.

More than this, we adjust the chi by introducing sources of chi, such as plants, reflect the chi and light with mirrors or shiny surfaces, change the chi and light through colours and create different spaces for chi to flow through, depending on how we furnish a room. In this sense, feng shui is an interplay between nature and interior spaces, using the many resources we have, when creating a home.

Ultimately we are trying to create a home where we can best succeed, where our life will flow in ways that bring deeper peace, happiness, love, confidence and reflection. Our home becomes our inspiration, support, motivation and resource to live our life to the full. In this sense planting a human in his or her home is similar to planting a plant in the ideal soil and sunlight.

Susanna has dedicated her life to feng shui. I have taught with her often and enjoyed our many discussions about feng shui. She has a beautiful, elegant approach to feng shui that is practical, supportive and helps anyone make improvements in life. This book presents feng shui in a methodical, logical manner that helps the reader understand feng shui and make real changes to their home.

I very much like the title of Feng Shui Flow, as flow is such an important part of feng shui and life in general. I wish you all the very best in applying feng shui to your life through this excellent book and enjoying the rewards of this life-changing subject.

Simon Brown

Simon is the chair of the Feng Shui Society, author of numerous books including The Feng Shui Bible, international feng shui teacher and consultant. His feng shui projects include those with British Airways, The Body Shop, Paris Airports, Heron Tower and many other large building projects.

Introduction

Jenny:

In December 2016 I was asked if I wanted to write a book about feng shui. Spontaneous as I am, I accepted immediately. After two minutes of reflection, I realized that I didn't have enough knowledge to fill an entire book. I contacted my feng shui teacher, and now good friend and colleague, Susanna Utbult, to invite her to the project. Since each of us had our own ambitions to write, our dreams could now become reality.

The first time I met Susanna was when she came to our home to do a feng shui consultation. Afterwards, my wife and I jokingly agreed that it would just be enough if Susanna herself sat in our home with us. Her warm radiance and the grounded feeling we experienced would suffice.

Shortly after this consultation, I decided to attend her classes at Nordic School of Feng Shui. I wanted to become a certified feng shui consultant in order to start a new career. It is one of the best decisions I have ever made. The knowledge I gained during the year of training changed me, my way of thinking and how I related to life. I could now put into words emotions I had not previously been able to describe. I now understood that my home is an extension of myself and that I'm able to influence

the way I feel. I have always liked my home to be organised and now I understood that this feeling was related to feng shui. I'm so happy and proud that I have the opportunity to share my knowledge with all of you. I hope you'll be inspired, have fun and appreciate the importance of good feng shui. If I can change my life, you can too.

Make your day a good one!
Jenny

Susanna:

My first encounter with feng shui was in 1998 during a ski holiday in Norway. Even though I was tired after a day on the slopes, I was having trouble falling asleep. Suddenly I remembered something I had read in a feng shui book a few days earlier. It was about mirrors in the bedroom: 'If you can see yourself in the mirror while you are lying in bed, it can interfere with your sleep'. I glanced at the large mirror on the wall. I could clearly see myself from the bunk bed. So, a little sceptical but desperate for a solution, I covered the mirror with a large towel and soon fell asleep. When I woke up the next morning, I remember thinking, 'Hmm… maybe there is something in feng shui after all?' A little seed of hope and delight was planted in my heart. I decided to find out more about feng shui and if it could help me feel better. Today, 20 years later, from the bottom of my heart I can speak my truth about feng shui. Yes, it has definitely helped me.

Feng shui has given me a sense of purpose and has played an important role in my life even in times of adversity. A few times I've tried to escape. Sometimes the work was too stressful, sometimes I met other people's resistance or other challenges. But, just when I'm ready to give up, it always ends up with me continuing. I have no tattoos on my body but feng shui has become tattooed in my heart.

Hugs, Susanna

What is feng shui?

Feng shui is not just one thing, but three things: a science, an art and a life philosophy. All in one. There is something for everyone in feng shui no matter what your interests are.

What can feng shui do for you and your home? We would dare to say that it can make all the difference in the world. It is usually said that good feng shui should be felt, but not seen. This means that visitors to your home will experience feelings of joy, comfort and beauty - without really knowing exactly why. Then you have done well.

Feng shui provides the most amazing toolbox you can imagine. The toolbox contains so much, yet it does not weigh a single gram and you can carry it everywhere for your entire life.

How are you feeling? Are you stressed? Probably you have many demands in your work life, family and leisure activities. Maybe you also have a house, garden and a car to take care of? The list can be endless, but where do you find your energy to cope? Your home is a place to feel safe and to recharge yourself. Unfortunately, the home can also create stress instead of peace of mind. Then good feng shui is what you need.

Do you lack energy, balance and motivation? The first thing to do is to take a look at your home. You might find the answer there. The home is an extension of yourself. A messy home reflects a messy inner life. You know how much better you feel after you have cleaned out a room or wardrobe. This demonstrates that your surroundings affect you and that you are in charge of your own wellbeing. Imagine how much more you can achieve when the entire toolbox of feng shui is used.

For us, it is not just about decorating the surface. When you use feng shui you work with balance, deeper thought and wisdom. You get beauty into the bargain. If you take care of your home, you take care of yourself. And vice versa.

Science

How does science fit in to feng shui? By measuring brain waves using EEG, you can prove that feng shui works. Your brain produces different kinds of waves depending on which room you are in and the conditions you find there. Good feng shui in a room creates calm and creative brainwaves and bad feng shui creates the opposite. You will notice the difference.

Art

Feng shui is sometimes called 'the art of placement' - how to place things so that they are perceived as beautiful and interesting. You have probably experienced the need to move things around and change things in one way or another. It's all about finding a balance - or even an imbalance - which makes it feel 'right'. Much of this you feel intuitively but it's also an art that can be developed.

In a wider perspective, the art of placement applies to houses and buildings in their environmental context. Everything that can be done in the large scale, can also be done in the small. This means that the theory behind feng shui works equally well whether you are arranging a city, a village, a castle, a house, furniture or things in a room. In other words, it works in any situation. That's why the tools of feng shui are so effective. They are not limited to specific areas, but can be used in different cultures around the world. The theory is still the same.

Philosophy

The philosophical idea of feng shui is about living in harmony with our surroundings. It is to understand that we are affected by everything around us: environment, colours, shapes, materials and people.

There is also the idea of going with the flow instead of fighting against it. For example following the rhythm of daylight, or finding the right time or the right day for different activities. The difference to your life is like swimming with the current instead of struggling against it.

Why feng shui?

'Do you have feng shui here in your living room?' was the question I *(Susanna)* received from a journalist.

She had apparently expected to find something spectacular when she stepped into my home and she was a little surprised when she found my home 'normal'.

Maybe she thought that feng shui only applied to new, modern and minimalist homes. Here I stood in my house, built in 1935 and in need of renovation, claiming that I had good feng shui. The truth is that everyone has feng shui - all the time.

The question should rather be: 'Do you have favourable or less favourable feng shui in your home?'

You are constantly affected by your surroundings, which means you cannot opt out of feng shui. It is always there - in your home, at work, in the city, in the country – everywhere. Therefore, it´s better to ask yourself: Is the feng shui I am exposed to favourable?' If you find challenges, you probably want to improve it. In short you can say that feng shui gives you guidelines for balancing your life.

"In short you can say that feng shui gives you guidelines for balancing your life."

Feng shui – luxury or everyday life?

Magazines and social media might give the impression that feng shui is only used in expensive interior design. But good feng shui can be created at no cost at all, because most of it is about using what you already have. Maybe you can move some things around or take some things out. Of course it can be fun to buy new things but it is absolutely not necessary. If you have to add anything it will usually be plants.

Feng shui in interior design is about finding a balance between colours, shapes and different materials to make the room feel comfortable and to make it suitable for the activities that take place in the room. A common misconception is that feng shui is the same as minimalism. The expression 'less is more' is an important principle of feng shui but only to a certain extent because it is also possible for a room to contain too few things. In a room that is too empty, the energy flows too quickly, the balance is disturbed and the comfortable feeling is lost.

Feng shui is not minimalism, an interior decoration style or a religion but a way of thinking while decorating in your chosen style. No matter what style you choose, feng shui is ageless. Since it originates in China, it contains traces of Eastern philosophy, tradition and culture.

You don't need trendy interior decoration to create harmony in your home. Impulse purchases can leave you unsatisfied. Essentially it is about being organised and keeping a good balance in the room.

So, the answer to the question is that feng shui is for everyday life, anybody and any budget.

PLANTS CAN:
» purify the air.
» increase humidity.
» raise the energy.
» calm the energy.
» balance the room.
» create safety.
» connect you with nature.

The toolbox

There are five basic tools when decorating with feng shui. Put simply, these are:

1. energy flow
2. security
3. contrast
4. colour, shape and material
5. energy enhancers

Using these five tools, you can create the ultimate interior. With experience, you will be able to work with all the tools at the same time, but for now you can use them one at a time. Let's take a look at the first tool.

TOOL 1 – ENERGY FLOW

Energy flows between doors and windows in every room. Their size and number as well as their position in relation to each other all affect the flow. The flow is also affected by the furniture and how they are placed, so you have to find the right proportion in relation to the room. Use your gut feeling.

A useful thing to remember is that 'energy moves as you do'. If you need to step between furniture and objects in a room, then the energy flow might be sluggish and you might want to make some changes. If there isn't enough furniture, you will experience emptiness and coldness in the room. This is because the energy moves too fast, there is nothing to slow it down. The key is to place the furniture in a strategic way to slow down the energy when it is too fast, or conversely, remove furniture to create a better flow where it is too slow. All rooms and all houses have their own individual conditions. There are no ready-made solutions in feng shui. Everything is personally created for the room, the house and whoever lives there. It provides interior design on a deeper level.

"Leave what is good, and focus instead on what you can make better."

Challenging rooms have:

» two or more doors.

» windows opposite each other.

» doors opposite each other.

» rooms that have an inward-pointing corner, such as L-shaped rooms.

Each room is unique, so to create a good energy flow each room needs its own solution. We do not want to sound negative and make a long list of problems but when it comes to feng shui it is actually more common to focus on the challenges and difficulties. We do 'troubleshooting'. Leave what is good, and focus instead on what you can make better. Or, as the saying goes, 'if it isn't broken, don't fix it'.

Avoid placing:

» A desk between the door and window - it can make you uneasy and you may lose focus when you sit there.

» A mirror facing the front door - it is uncomfortable to confront your own reflection when you open your door; also, the incoming energy tends to bounce out again.

» Pictures in descending height on a staircase wall - the energy accelerates downwards and there is more risk that you might fall when you walk down the stairs.

"Find the balance:
not too low and and not too tall,
not too big and not too small."

Here is a story to help you remember what we've talked about:

Imagine a stream in the forest where the water flows around some stones. Some are smooth and some are rough. The round shape allows the water to pass easily. The angular stones create turbulence and disrupt the flow of water. Pile up a lot of stones in the same place and the flow will stop. The water stagnates. On the other hand, if you remove all the stones from the stream, the water will flow too quickly. The stream is no longer a place of peace.

Whatever you do with the stones in the stream, it will affect the flow and the energy. To keep the calm and comfortable feeling you need to make sure you have the right amount of stones in the stream. Find the balance - not too many and and not too few, not too big and not too small. We also need both round and angular shapes to get a diverse dynamic in the flow. Then you can sit by your stream and feel good.

Now apply the principle of this story, where the stones are your furniture and the water is the energy that moves through your home.

TOOL 2 – SECURITY

The second tool in feng shui is security. To feel good and to focus on the activities you want to do in the room you need to feel safe. Security is a primitive need that lies deep in our genes. As long as humans have lived on earth, this need has existed. Originally, it was a question of survival by placing a shelter or house where strong winds and water did not destroy the home, and kept the inhabitants alert to approaching threats. In feng shui this primitive need for security is called power position. You hold your power if you sit with a sturdy back, support on the sides and a free view in front of you. Then no one can surprise you from behind because you can see everyone who comes into the room. You are in control of the room, the situation and your own power. This key principle should be used in every room and every situation. Whether you are sitting, standing or lying, the power position makes you feel comfortable.

You find the power position by looking for the wall that is the most complete. If there is a wall that lacks doors and windows, this is probably the best wall to give you the power position. Place the main sitting or sleeping furniture here. In a study you should place the desk so you sit with the power wall behind you. Regardless of the room, to feel safe, you need to see the door. In a room where many people are sitting, not everyone is likely to get an equally good power position. The goal is to find good seating for as many people as possible and to arrange the furniture in a balanced and functional way.

Other less favourable situations:

It's not just when you sit with your back to the door. There are a number of other situations that can create feelings of insecurity, although you might not be aware of it, as it can happen unconsciously.

Heavy and threatening feelings can be caused by:

» a shelf over the bed or sofa with heavy books and ornaments

» a crystal chandelier in the ceiling above the bed

» a large picture on the wall above the bed or sofa

You can also feel insecure when you are in a room with several doors which means you have to be in control of many different directions at the same time. Anything that makes the room insecure and disturbing can easily be changed into a room that feels safe and positive.

TOOL 3 – CONTRASTS

The black and white symbol describing yin and yang is now well known but for some it still feels mystifying and unfamiliar. The simple explanation is that life consists of contrasts, and can be described by words such as:

» sun – moon

» day - night

» high - low

» big - small

» light - dark

» active - passive

» hungry - satisfied

» happy - sad

The list can be endless…

Look around one of your rooms and you will see things that can be described in words like: straight -round, large pattern - small pattern, white - black, hard - soft etc. You have different numbers of things, some are even while others are odd. Just as contrasts create balance in life, contrasts are needed to create a beautiful room. In feng shui, this tool is called yin and yang, where yin stands for what is small, soft and dark and yang stands for what is large, hard and bright, for example. Your brain likes to have fun, which means it needs to be a little challenged. A room that lacks contrasts is perceived as boring and unbalanced. Instead, try to find things that excite the eye and brain. Now the room has life and you perceive it as beautiful and comfortable. You can for example place:

» high next to low

» broad next to narrow

» straight next to curved

» bright next to dark

» large patterns next to small

» older furniture mixed with more modern furniture

and so on ...

Yin & Yang

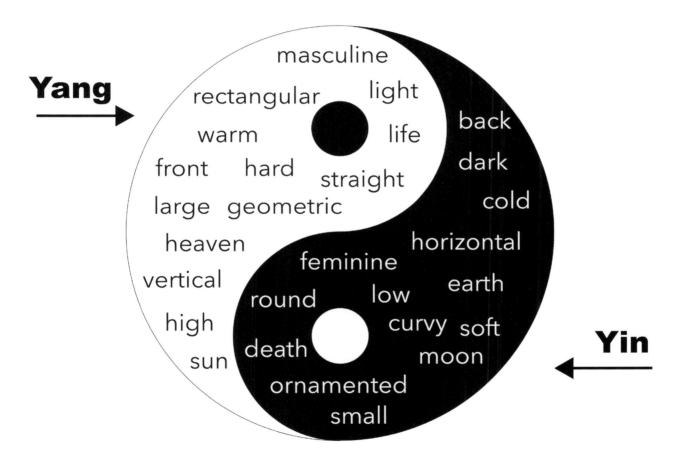

Yang →

masculine
rectangular light
warm life
front hard
straight
large geometric
heaven feminine horizontal
vertical earth
round low
high curvy soft
sun death moon
ornamented
small

back
dark
cold

Yin ←

Straight and angular furniture gives yang energy. To get more yin energy and more balance to the room, add, for example, soft pillows, a round mat and green plants. An ornate crystal chandelier becomes more beautiful if it hangs above a table and chairs that have straight lines because they have contrasting energies. A crystal chandelier over a table and chairs with softly-curved legs and intricately-carved backrests might seem boring, as they have the same energy. Similarly, it becomes more interesting if you place a round table on a rectangular mat or vice versa. When the same shape is repeated several times, it is perceived as boring and predictable.

Odd and even numbers

Just as you seek contrasts in colour, shape and pattern, your brain also wants to be stimulated when it comes to how many things are placed together. An even number of things gives a calm impression (yin) while an uneven number makes the feeling more active (yang). You may have two plants of the same kind in pots of the same style on your windowsill. This gives calmness and stability to the room (yin). If you want the windowsill to feel exciting and stimulating (yang) instead, you should have an odd number of things at different heights and with different shapes.

A windowsill doesn't have to be adorned with just plants. You should arrange plants, lamps and ornaments together in a harmonious composition. Find contrasting shapes and sizes so that some are yin and the others are yang.

"To live with dis-harmony creates dis-ease
To live with harmony creates ease."

TOOL 4 – COLOUR, SHAPE AND MATERIAL

Different materials give you different experiences. A sheepskin feels warm, untreated boards feel warmly dry, metal is cold, grass feels freshly moist, while water is wet and often cold. Everything around you has a different energy, whether we talk about colour, shape or material. This is why you experience them so differently.

The different energy patterns are called the five elements. We can also say 'building blocks of the universe' because everything in the universe belongs to one of the five elements: wood, fire, earth, metal and water. These eastern elements are different from the four elements used by Greek philosophers.

Colour is often the first thing you notice when you enter a room. If the room mostly contains white - white walls, white ceiling, white floor and white furniture - you will experience a very large amount of the element metal. A seventies-style cabin with pine on the walls, ceilings, floors and furniture provides an overflow of the earth element. These two rooms are both imbalanced.

When one or more elements are missing, it feels as if the room is not 'finished'. (You can also get the same feeling when it comes to the contrasts we talked about earlier). It is only when you have all five elements in the room together with a good combination of contrasts that the room feels balanced. Balance creates harmony.

The image on the left lacks the wood element and has too much earth, while the image on the right has a better balance of elements as well as more contrast through the dark pillows.

Fire element

All sources of light - sunlight, lamps, oil lamps, candles and fireplaces.
The red colour spectrum.
Animals and human beings.
Things from animals, such as fur, bone, feathers, wool, silk.
Art/items depicting animals, human beings, sunlight or fire.
Triangles, pyramids and cone shapes.

Wood element

Green colours (sometimes turquoise).
Plants, cotton, linen, viscose.
Column shapes and stripes.
Items/art/fabric/wallpaper depicting landscapes, flowers and plants.

Earth element

Sand, bricks, tiles, concrete and ceramics.
Squares and horizontal rectangles.
Earth colours and yellows (except fire-yellow).
Items made of natural unpainted wood are generally considered to be earth element.

Water element

Black, blue, very dark colours.
Wave shapes, swirling shapes and patterns.
Glass and cut crystal.
Reflective surfaces and mirrors.
Water features.
Art depicting water.

Metal element

Metals, metal colours, white and pale pastel colours.
Mountains and large rocks.
Uncut crystals.
Items/art made of metal.
Circles, ovals and arches.

All elements should be represented in each room and well balanced with each other. Then how can you know when you have found the balance? You might think that equal amounts of each element creates balance, but it's not that easy. All elements have different intensities and therefore different proportions create a balance.

A good guideline would be:

» mostly earth

» a good deal of wood and metal

» a little bit of water

» and least of all, a touch of fire

Example 1:

» brown floor (earth)

» white ceiling and walls (metal)

» green plants (wood)

» black sofa (water)

» bright pink pillows on the sofa (fire)

Example 2:

» brown floor (earth)

» white sofa (metal)

» large green mat (wood)

» black coffee table (water)

» red roses in a vase on the coffee table (fire)

Items in a room will probably consist of more than one element. Let your intuition guide you to find the most dominant element.

There is not just one single solution and no right or wrong when it comes to balancing a room. There are many combinations of colours, shapes and materials that provide balance. Start with the things you really want to keep. Identify which elements these items represent. What do you need more of? What do you need to take away? Use your gut feeling. Is it too bright? Maybe you need to add something darker, or is it better to add more plants? Keep asking yourself questions like this. Add or remove until you feel content. Then the room is ready. If you find it difficult, it gets easier the more you do it.

Compatible partners

Every detail in your room consists of different elements. The colour provides one element, the shape another and the material a third. Sometimes these three elements are one and the same and sometimes they are different. Use your feelings to identify the dominant element, the one that 'speaks most to you'. You usually perceive the colour first, then the shape and then the material last.

Imagine a white round table on a square black mat:

Table, the five elements:
» colour – white; element – metal
» shape – round; element – metal

Table, yin and yang:
» white – yang because it's bright
» round – yin because it has a soft shape

Carpet, the five elements:
» colour – black; element – water
» shape – square; element – earth

Carpet, yin and yang:
» black – yin because it's dark
» square – yang because it has an angular shape

The two tools - the five elements and yin and yang - always work together. They are two different tools but are impossible to separate. Everything contains yin and yang as well as the five elements.

The five elements and yin and yang are expressed in colour, shape and material. When you focus on the five elements of a room, the colour speaks to you first. When you focus on the contrasts (yin and yang) the shapes will appear first. Therefore you always have to take both into consideration.

TOOL 5 – ENERGY ENHANCERS

A dark room lacks energy because light is energy. This is when you need help from one or more energy boosters. Imagine a room where the blinds are closed during the day. Your first reaction is to open the blinds and let the daylight in. As soon as light flows in, you have increased the energy in the room.

The sun is a source of energy for all life on earth and lack of daylight can damage our health. In the evenings and cloudy days we need to add extra light such as lamps, fires and candles.

Examples of energy enhancers:

» daylight, lamps, fires and candles

» houseplants and flowers

» fruit and vegetables

» water, such as an indoor water feature, an aquarium, a painting depicting images of water

» people, pets, TV or computer with moving images

» musical instruments, music, recorded sounds from nature

» mirrors

» symbols which hold personal meaning

Fresh, fresh, fresh

» all plants and flowers should be fresh and healthy

» all water in aquariums, bowls and vases should be clean

» moving water stays fresh longer than still water

» only use undamaged mirrors and remember to keep them clean

"When you take care of your home, you take care of yourself."

Guidelines for mirrors:

» square mirrors should have frames

» use a round mirror if you don't want a frame

» avoid mirror walls and other arrangements that give a split image

» place the mirror at the right height for its purpose

» make sure the mirror reflects something positive for you (e.g. a vase of flowers, not laundry)

Corner + plant = true love

Energy easily becomes stagnant in dark corners. This is easily remedied by putting a plant there. Moving things around by trial and error to work out a balance is exciting and inspiring. You feel the result immediately.

Clear the clutter

Positive energy - two wonderful words that give hope and good feelings. You can largely create positive energy yourself. It's all about how the energy flows in your home. The state of the room is contagious and your environment affects you. We have mentioned before that everything is energy and that your home is an extension of yourself. It also reflects you and how you feel. Tidy home, tidy mind. By analysing the energy in your home, you can make plans for positive change.

How does it work?

By drawing a parallel between feng shui and acupuncture, it is easy to understand that you are affected by your own mess. When you are in pain somewhere in your body, it is a sign of a blockage. When this happens, energy and blood cannot flow as freely as they should. The acupuncturist stimulates blood and energy flow and your pain goes away. Your home works in the same way. Piles of mess or rooms filled with junk, for example, create a block in the home and ... the home is you. If the energy cannot flow in your home, it means that you are the one who suffers.

Therefore, set aside time to declutter, so that the positive energy is released. Clearing old stagnant energy allows new energy to flow into you.

Getting started

» start in the entrance hall

» continue to the room where you have the most clutter

» don't do everything at the same time: take one box at a time, one wardrobe at a time and so on

» create a memory box for the most precious memories

» keep the things you love, if you have space for them

» give away gifts you no longer want or need

» ask other people to give you the gifts you actually want or need

» give things away - giving feels good!

» sell things online or in markets

» if you feel unsure about an item, give it some time and come back to it later

» if you do have to throw something away, recycle

We don't want you to throw everything away, just clear the clutter, look at each item and notice your feelings about it. Just keep the things you like, need or use. Make sure everything has its own place.

Sometimes it has to get worse before it gets better. You may have to pull out old things from their hiding places and spread them across the floor. It may look like a compete mess, but it is actually a positive start.

Feelings

Clearing the clutter can be wonderful, but it could also stir up unwanted feelings and memories. You can feel exhausted after clearing out the belongings of someone who is no longer with you. Some things might be associated with guilt. Maybe you have inherited something from a loved relative and you do not have the heart to throw it away. You might not like that gift from your aunt, but you bring it out every time she visits. But don't fill your home with things you don't like, because they will drain you of energy. Clearing out can be emotional, but you will feel better afterwards.

Here are some decluttering guidelines.

Hallway:
» identical clothes hangers look better

» keep shoes on a shelf away from the floor

» keep shoes on a (shoe) shelf or in a shoe cabinet

» if possible, store things in cupboards

Children's rooms:
» help children organise their own things

» tell them that 'everything lives somewhere'

» tell them that everything has its place

Computer:
» organise photos into different categories

» clear your inbox

» use folders

» have as little as possible on the computer desktop

Home office:
» put your pens in a pot

» put documents into folders and files

» arrange binders and books on your shelf according to colour

» put dark files on lower shelves, and light ones higher up

Kitchen:
» defrost your freezer

» clear food cupboards and fridge

» wash up and clean the surfaces after every meal (looking at the mess uses more energy than doing it straight away)

Bathroom:

» reduce the number of products you have

» clean the sink often

» put a green plant in the bathroom

Living room:

» give the bookshelf a clear structure, group books by colour (as you did in your office)

» place dark books and boxes at the bottom of the bookshelf and light ones at the top

» be selective about what you keep in your room (ornaments, pictures etc.)

Colours

What you perceive as colour is in fact energy (electromagnetic radiation), where every colour vibrates with its own frequency. In feng shui we use the colours of the five elements to balance a room, but there is also a psychological aspect to colour that is sometimes forgotten. For example, in basic feng shui you might be advised to paint your walls green in the east or south-east part of your home. But if this area is a work space, the green, from a colour-psychological point of view, would not be so so helpful. Many shades of green make you so calm and relaxed that you can lose focus. Green is also a special colour because, lying in the middle of the spectrum, it is considered to be balanced and neutral. Sometimes the colours of the five elements work well with colour psychology and at other times they do not. The secret is to be able to combine these two ways of using colour.

Simply explained:

» you will feel alert with red, yellow, orange and lime green

» you will feel calm with blue, green, purple and brown

» green is neutral and can be either invigorating or calming depending on the shade

The colour of your walls, ceilings and floors have a huge impact as there are large surfaces. White is often the best colour for the ceiling because it gives the room light and space. The height of the ceiling is also important. If your ceiling is low it can feel oppressive, paint it white and the change is dramatic. High ceilings painted white, on the other hand, are unlikely to make you feel cosy. Height is impressive in a cathedral, but not in your home where you want to feel warm and safe.

THE IMPACT OF COLOUR

Red: Use red with caution. This is the most powerful colour and represents the fire element. No room should be completely red, but red splashes could be exactly what a room needs. In a theatre, red chairs and curtains are perfect because this colour stands for drama, love and passion. In your home, red works best as an accent colour and for adding fire elements to a room.

Pink: Soft pink is motherly and comforting. Therefore, it's good to have a pink blanket handy. Pink encourages kindness and has been shown to calm aggression in some prisons. If you are ill or having a difficult time, you may feel drawn to the motherly embrace of soft pink in clothing or decor.

Orange: This is a social colour that stimulates appetite and digestion, making it a good colour for kitchens and dining rooms. Large expanses of orange may not be so popular today, but as an accent colour it can be fine. If you want its positive effect without painting the walls orange, you can have a large bowl of oranges, orangecoloured plates and mugs, table cloths or curtains that provide a smaller dose of the colour. An exposed terracotta-coloured brick wall can be stylish and gives your kitchen or dining room just the right effect and feeling.

Yellow: The colour of the sun gives you warmth. The heat makes you relaxed and sociable. Yellow is therefore perfect for rooms where you want people to talk and open up, whether it is in a meeting room at work, a living room, or a kitchen for relaxed dinner parties. Yellow also stimulates the intellect so it works better in the office where you want to keep your brain focused rather than in the bedroom where you want to rest.

Green: This colour is considered neutral since it is in the middle of the colour spectrum. Like the green of nature it can give you energy when you need a boost, and it can help calm you when you need to relax. Like all colours, different shades will provide different effects.

A light green gives energy and alertness, whereas soft olive green is more calming and relaxing. Shade always matters, whatever colour you choose. In general, though, green is not the best colour for walls in a work space or kitchen cabinets, but in a bedroom or a room for relaxation it could be just perfect.

Blue: This is the colour of calm and cool. This makes it unsuitable for rooms designed for social gatherings but works quite well in the bedroom. Avoid overdoing it because too much blue can make you depressed and worried. All bedrooms also need heat to keep the flame of love alive, so remember to bring some warmth by also adding other elements. Blue and white in a kitchen is a classic colour scheme with both pros and cons. Blue inhibits bacterial growth, which is good in a kitchen, but it is not only bacteria that is inhibited, but also the appetite.

Purple: According to colour psychology, purple is associated with calm, meditation, inspiration, the arts and spirituality. You will probably find it difficult to cope with large amounts of purple as it can dominate the room but as an accent colour it is perfect.

Brown: This is associated with 'mother earth' and fills you with calmness. Brown is therefore suitable on the floor because it gives a grounded and safe feeling. If your walls are brown, however, the room seems smaller because the colour is dark. A brown ceiling feels oppressive unless it is very high. On the other hand, a bedroom in brown, beige or 'skin tones' can be just the quiet and safe place you longed for.

Beige / Offwhite: Beige and offwhite are often used as a neutral base as they do not have as much energy and provide a quiet background to the rest of the room.

Grey: Like beige, grey has very little energy and could also be used as a neutral base. Grey is a mixture of black and white. It is the colour of compromise and does not draw so much attention. Instead it enhances all other colours so that they can shine. Grey is a sober and stylish colour that suits all rooms as long as it is also balanced with accent colour and other elements.

Black: According to physics, black is not a colour but it is the absence of light, in other words, lack of energy. It is therefore easy for black rooms to seem less energetic and black furniture tends to dominate a room. Black absorbs light and can easily take over, therefore it should not appear on too many details in the room which can leave you feeling scattered. Black is a bit mysterious, quiet and sensual, something that every room needs - in small doses.

White: Physics tells us that white is also not a colour, but white objects fully reflect and scatter all other colours. In the Nordic countries there has been a long-standing trend to decorate homes entirely in white, which has resulted in a severe imbalance between the elements. Fortunately, the trend has now changed and more colours can be seen in homes.

Colour your home using the colours you need right now in order to feel good. For example, if you are in a stressful period, be careful of using strong colours. If you need motivation to start new projects, surround yourself with lively green tones and lots of white. Ask yourself which phase in life you're in right now, and decorate your home accordingly.

Neutral base: No matter what the current trend is, it's still quite practical to have a neutral base colour on the large surfaces such as walls. They can be white, off-white, beige or light grey. See your home as a blank canvas where you can easily change colours and style depending on what inspires you at the moment.

Accent colour: To make the room interesting and beautiful, you need to create an eye-catching accent colour that contrasts with the wall colour and flooring. Add the accent colour to furniture, carpets, cushions, curtains and other details. If you have the accent colour in three different places in the room, it will feel well-designed rather than random. Adding it to more than three places the room can be perceived as scattered. Decorating this way is simpler, more environmentally friendly and sustainable than repainting or wallpapering when the mood or trend changes.

Everything that is positive about a colour can also turn to a negative when you have too much of it. For example:

	Positive	Negative
Red:	love, sex, strength, courage, success	drama, anger, frustration, feeling too warm
Orange:	stimulates appetite and digestion, sociability	excessive talkativeness and sociability
Yellow:	stimulates intellect, promotes conversation, sociabililty	difficulties with relaxation, excessively talkative
Green:	calming, balancing, renewing	lack of motivation
Blue:	stress reducing, projecting trust and confidence	depressed, unable to socialise, indecisive
Pink:	mothering and caring	weak and unconfident
Purple:	calm, meditative, spiritual, artistic	too quiet
Brown:	stable, calm, caring	slow and resistant to change
Black:	quiet, sensual, mysterious	low energy, grief, jealousy
Grey:	sober, self-restrained, independent	self-critical, lifeless, unsociable
White:	purity, innocence, alertness, focus	rigid, pedantic, withdrawn

Our tips for sustainability

Living space
Do you really need all the space you have today? Is it time to move somewhere smaller? Maybe you could move somewhere that is easier to maintain and heat.

Repair, don't throw away
Even mobiles and computers are often repairable at a reasonable price.

Cleaning
Clean naturally and sustainably with, for example, lemon, vinegar, salt and bicarbonate.

Heating
Lower the temperature in your home. Light candles, wear slippers and a warm sweater. It's cosy, and increases alertness.

Laundry
Dry your laundry outdoors when the weather permits.

Cooking
Make some extra food for the next day or for freezing.

Treasures

When you buy furniture and items for decoration, first check the second hand and vintage shops. You can find fantastic treasures.

Water

Avoid running water when you wash the dishes and brush your teeth.

Shopping

When you buy something new, think sustainably: less plastic and more environmentally-friendly materials.

Fuel

Leave the car at home and take the bike when you can, and also get some routine exercise.

Plastic

Say 'no thank you' to plastic bags and use your own reusable one.

Paper

Choose electronic bills and don't print anything you don't have to.

Swapping

Arrange a shelf at work where you can exchange books and other belongings.

And finally, of course...

Reuse or upcycle as much as possible.

Entrance

The front door and the hallway is the most important part of your home. This is where most of the energy comes in. According to feng shui, the front door is like a mouth, where all the important energy enters. If we can see the front door as a symbolic mouth, the hallway is the throat. This is the route by which you take in air and nourishment. If the throat is blocked, you will choke. It's the same in your home: if your hall is blocked with clothes, shoes or other clutter, the energy will stop there without going into your home, which will then end up without fresh energy.

The entrance gives your guests their first impression and sets the tone for the rest of your home. The most important thing is that the entrance is welcoming, unblocked and a joy to come home to.

If another door or a window is aligned with your entrance door, so that when you enter you can see out of the other side of your home, the risk is that the energy will flow straight through without staying inside. Slow down the flow with the help of things appropriate to this room such as curtains, furniture, carpets or plants. Be careful with long narrow carpets, which speed up the energy even more. In this case, a round or square rug is better.

Things that make the hall welcoming:
» lighting
» plants
» pleasant scent
» good organisation
» sufficient storage
» personal items (e.g. family photos)

"The entrance gives your guests their first impression and sets the tone for the rest of your home."

The hallway is a place where clothes and shoes can easily overflow. Only keep in the open what you use on a daily basis. Closed storage gives a calmer impression of the hallway.

Most people want to have a mirror in the hallway, but avoid placing it facing the front door. Energy flowing in is reflected in the mirror and bounces back out again. Besides, it can be startling to meet your own image when you open your front door. However, it's good to put beautiful things in front of a mirror. This way ten tulips, for example, will be perceived as twenty and so on. Remember to place the mirror at the right height so it will suit everybody who's using it.

According to feng shui, a large and bright hallway is desirable, although this is quite hard to find. Often you need to work with your hallway to make it seem brighter and larger than it is. Dark walls make the hallway appear smaller and light walls give a feeling of space. A long and narrow hallway might appear wider if you paint light walls along the sides and a darker wall at the end of the passage. Use carpets with stripes that run across, rather than along, the hallway. A round rug can also make the hall appear wider.

When you are starting to use feng shui in your home, our advice is always to start with the entrance and the hallway.

Bedroom

The bedroom is a space where privacy is important. Like the entrance, it's good to be neat, tidy and clutter free in this room. The bedroom tends to be the clutter room, because other people don't usually see it. You spend a lot of your time here - one third of your life. This makes the bedroom incredibly important, as the place where you rest your body and soul. That's why you want this room to be organised and well ordered.

Cosy and soft

A bedroom should be cosy, warm and soft when it comes to colours, shapes and materials. Avoid things that feel cold and hard and go for softness instead.

If possible, place the bed with the head against a solid wall and so you can see the door. To be in control of the room gives you a feeling of security. Some rooms are better as bedrooms than others. The best bedrooms are those with just one door and not too many windows. These 'openings' create flow and movement. For example, a room with two doors will divide your focus and your sleep may be disturbed. Avoid placing the bed with the head against a window as this is an insecure position.

A headboard is more important than you might think. It adds to the feeling of security. It's important that the headboard is the right height. It should be in proportion to the size of your bed which means that a single bed should have a lower headboard compared to a wider one.

» bedside lamps are best placed at the side on a bedside table
» bedside tables which are lower than the bed look out of proportion
» bedside tables which are higher than the bed will point a sharp edge towards you

The perfect bedside table should be the same height as the bed. Then it doesn't matter if you have a sharp edge as this sharp energy is directed into the mattress.

"The perfect bedside table should be the same height as the bed."

Things that could disturb your sleep:

sleeping on curry lines (geopathic stress)*

sleeping under a sloped ceiling

having a large and heavy ceiling light above your bed

» a bedside table which is too high with sharp edges

» a missing headboard

» a headboard which is too high or too low

» a headboard that is too hard, such as wood or metal

» reading lamps, shelves and heavy pictures above your head

Better sleep

Try to keep electronics, such as TV, computers and mobile phones outside the bedroom as much as you can. Many appliances give out radiation around you and it's unnecessary to expose yourself during the night. The dose you have during the day is enough.

Some people say mirrors in the bedroom are a no-no, but we don't. As long as you can't see yourself in the mirror while you are lying in bed, it's OK. To feel more secure, it's important to see the door while you are lying in bed. A mirror could be used like a rear-view mirror if your bed is in an awkward position. If you have a large wall mirror or maybe a group of mirrors on your wardrobe, you can easily make the room calm by covering them at night. Hang up a curtain rail in the ceiling and hang beautiful fabrics that you pull across at night.

*Curry lines are energy lines (geopathic stress) that can lead to both poor sleep and bad health.

Storage

It's common to have wardrobes in your bedroom. Ideally, clothes and bed linen should be kept in a separate closet outside the bedroom.

According to feng shui, it's good if the energy can also flow under the bed. Lots of storage under your bed creates a blockage in the energy flow and the serene feeling in the room is lost. What you store under the bed can also affect you. Avoid items connected to work, belongings which have strong personal significance, or things that belong in the past, for example love letters.

If your home is very small, you may have to compromise. For example you can store bed linen and extra blankets under the bed, as these are still connected with sleeping.

Colour in the bedroom

As well as being affected by colour through the five elements, you are also influenced on a psychological level. Therefore it is good to have colours on the bedroom walls which provide you with peace and calm. Active colours, such as red, yellow and orange, will keep you alert while you are trying to sleep. Instead, choose calm and secure colours in earthy shades, such as beiges or browns but also soft pinks. White, grey, green, blue and purple can also be suitable for bedrooms. It is the intensity of the colour which determines how you are affected. An intense colour could belong to one element and have a certain energy, but a more diluted and softer shade changes the energy.

Symbols

Everything in your bedroom symbolises your love relationship. Take a look at what your pictures and ornaments are really showing you. Are they in line with what you want in your relationship? Symbols of love often come in pairs. Two plants on the window sill, two lamps, two cushions on the bed, can symbolise being a couple.

Bedside tables on both sides of the bed give balance both to the relationship and the room. Most importantly when it comes to symbols is that you choose them yourself. Symbols remind you of what you want to achieve, so pick items which really talk to your heart.

➲ Pictures

Choose pictures carefully. Pictures of children and family are great, but not in the bedroom as they can get in the way of your relationship and private life.

➲ Scents

Scents affect you at a deep level. The smell of newly-washed bed linen is wonderful. You can also use lavender oil together with a diffuser, as lavender aids sleep.

➲ Plants

Some feng shui practitioners believe that the bedroom should be free from plants. The reason for this is that plants provide oxygen using photosynthesis during daytime but absorb oxygen at night. Orchids are an exception. That's why the orchid has become a popular bedroom plant.

In our opinion, all rooms need plants because balance in the room is more important than the small loss of oxygen.

➲ Work

Never bring work into your bedroom. Stress related to your work will disturb your sleep and relaxation.

➲ Sleep Tips

Try to relax for an hour before going to bed. If you usually exercise in the evenings, do this as early as possible so you have time to wind down before it's time to sleep. Light candles, play soft music, avoid watching a disturbing movie or using social media. In other words, create a harmonious atmosphere and make your evening as relaxed as you can. Remember to put out all your candles before you go to bed.

Avoid:

» red bed linen if you have trouble sleeping (red does not promote good sleep)

» using your mobile phone as an alarm clock due to radiation (flight mode is better)

» going to bed with an unresolved conflict with your partner

It's good to:

» use bed linen made of natural fabric (cotton, linen, silk)

» put your feet on something soft and warm when you get up (rug or slippers)

» have an adjustable reading lamp beside your bed in addition to your bedside lamp

The Kitchen

The kitchen contains two parts. One is active, where you are inspired to work and cook, and the other is inactive, where you relax and enjoy your food. The kitchen is often considered the 'heart of your home', a place where you spend a lot of time whether you are on your own, with family or friends. It's important that you feel at home in your kitchen and keep it organised.

Important questions to ask yourself:

» what feeling do you get from your kitchen?

» do you feel inspired to cook?

» do you feel energised and want to create new dishes?

» can you relax and spend time here?

» do you like eating in this space?

» do you want to be sociable here?

» is this a place to gather the family?

Kitchen Colours

It is easier to be inspired in a bright kitchen rather than in a dark one. The layout of the kitchen and the light through the windows play a big part in inspiring you to cook. Light is energy, and darkness is absence of energy, so it's easy to feel unmotivated if it's too dark. Good colours for your kitchen could, for example, be white or light grey. Kitchen cabinets take up a lot of space so if you choose dark ones it's easy to lose energy and motivation. Black cupboards can be very stylish, but you need to balance them with light and lighter colours in the rest of the kitchen.

Check out your kitchen. What does it look like in your:

» fridge

» freezer

» cupboards

» drawers

» storage areas

Don't forget your:

» sink

» kitchen top

» kitchen table

…these areas also need to be clean and fresh

Stay organised and make sure everything has its own place. It's easier if everybody knows in which drawer or cupboards they can find utensils. You avoid unnecessary irritation and you can put your energy into something else.

Go through old cookbooks and recipes. It's liberating to clear out, recycle or give away what you no longer want. Clean cupboards and clear out products which are not used or which have passed their best before date.

Check on a regular basis what you have in the fridge, the freezer and your food cupboard, so you know everything is fresh and usable. Also organise the cleaning cupboard and the recycling area.

Cooking inspiration

Try to keep stressful things away from the kitchen, for example TV, computers and mobile phones, which can take your focus away from cooking. A chef in harmony makes tastier food.

Power position

It might be a challenge to find the power position in the kitchen. The power position is needed when you do the dishes, cook, work in the preparation area and when you are sitting at the kitchen table. You might need one or two compromises to make this work. If there is enough space, a kitchen island is often a good solution. You will then be able to face the room when you work and you can see if somebody comes in.

A solution for a small kitchen could be to place a mirror above the sink to reflect the room. It might sound like a strange piece of advice, but it could make a big difference to be in control of what's happening behind you. In addition the kitchen will feel bigger and lighter.

Things that can disturb you in the kitchen:

» to sit or stand on Curry lines*

» to be unable to see the door

» clutter or disorganisation

» too many patterns, colours and items which over stimulate you visually

» bad smells

➲ Pictures and symbols

Avoid abstract art on the kitchen walls so your subconscious mind doesn't have to interpret the symbolism of the picture. It's better to focus on the food and the eating. Pictures with food and nature work well since there is a natural connection with the kitchen.

➲ Scents

Nice smells feel good. Not much beats the smell of freshly-baked buns or good food. The kitchen stays fresh by changing the bin bags regularly.

*Curry lines are energy lines which can lead to bad concentration and poor health.

➲ Plants

Plants belong to the wood element and have an aspiring energy which is alert and fresh. A few plants on the window sill are a good way of getting some wood energy into the kitchen. The kitchen is dominated by fire (the stove) and water (the tap). To create balance, you could place potted herbs, for example basil, in a terracotta pot by the sink. It looks stylish and feels harmonious since the wood and earth elements are often underrepresented here.

➲ Work

The kitchen table often doubles as a workspace, when you don't have a separate study room. It's important to take away the items associated with work or study when you sit down to eat. You will then be able to eat mindfully rather than being reminded of work.

KITCHEN TIPS

Put away telephones and other devices to stay sociable and focused during your meal. Light candles, turn off the TV. Instead, play soft music to create a harmonious and comfortable atmosphere. Take your time to be calm and relaxed. This is the perfect moment to gather the whole family, to talk and review the day. A round table makes it easier to keep the peace and to have conversations.

Avoid:

» a clock on the kitchen wall and let the meal be timeless

» knives displayed on a magnetic strip (they're sharp and threatening)

» green walls and cupboards in the work area of the kitchen

It's good to have:

» wood and earth elements close to the sink

» knives hidden in a block

» a round or oval kitchen table

Remember:

» blue colours reduce your appetite

» orange stimulates the appetite and digestion

The Living Room

The living room is where the whole family like to come together. It's also a room which should be flexible. It must work both for a nap on the sofa as well as playing a game, watching TV, reading or even eating, since some living rooms also include a dining area.

In the living room, you probably like to relax and take it easy. Soft furniture makes you relaxed, so a three piece suite is usually a good starting point. Place the furniture so that they create a group, as they belong together and 'talk to each other'. The most common placement for the sofa is against the wall without windows or doors to secure the power position. Cover the couch with cushions and throws to make it soft and cosy. Curtains and carpets also add softness, and it's a good way of bringing in different elements depending on which colours, shapes and materials you choose for these items.

The TV

Although the TV nowadays has to make way for all the computers and devices, a lot of people still choose to have a big TV in the living room. The most common mistake is putting the TV on the wall which doesn't have windows and doors. Instead the couch should go here. Otherwise you end up watching TV with a door behind you leaving you less secure and not in a power position. You will not see if somebody enters the room. Also, the TV is not the most beautiful or inviting thing to welcome you when you first enter the living room. One of the biggest keys to creating a beautiful and cosy feeling is finding the right wall to place the sofa against. Give the sofa the starring role and the TV a less prominent part to make the room much more beautiful and comfortable to spend time in.

Colour in the living room

Choose neutral colours for your walls if you easily want to change style according to trend, inspiration or season. No matter which neutral colour you choose, you will still have to add the other elements to balance the room. You can easily do it while choosing furniture, carpets, curtains and other accessories to complement the colour of the walls. If you wish to have a sociable living room, where it's easy to talk and easy to relax, you should choose warm colours as a base. Warmth relaxes and opens you while cold closes you up. All colours can be both cold and warm. Warm colours have yellow undertones, while cold colours have underlying blue tones.

Challenges in the living room

» sitting on Curry lines*

» an oppressive feeling under a sloped ceiling or beams

» a lamp hanging too low so it hides the person you want to talk to

» sofa and armchairs without armrests

» dark corners

» finding the right combination of lighting for different activities

Contrasts

If you, for example, choose a grey round carpet for your grey round table, it will look boring since both the colour and the shape are repeated. You brain will then lack stimulus. If you instead choose a square carpet in a different colour you have created contrast with colour and shape. How to use yin and yang is one of the secrets behind an interesting, harmonious and balanced room.

Remember

» big room - big furniture

» small room - compact furniture

» large window - large plants

» small window - smaller plants

» boring corners - place a plant or a light (or both)

» many small black details in a room create a messy feeling

*Curry lines are energy lines which can interfere with relaxation and health.

➲ Art

Only have pictures and symbols which give you a good feeling and which symbolise what you really want to attract and what you want to achieve. Decorate your walls with things that make you happy.

➲ Windows

In order to create an interesting window use contrasts, for example an uneven number of things, different heights, and different objects. If there is room for several plants, choose plants with different heights and different growth patterns (see the chapter about yin and yang). Don't be afraid to put other things on the window sill - a lamp and/or an ornament could be perfect to balance the plants. If you find it hard to find items of different heights, put books under some of the objects. Then you have created different levels and the window looks more interesting.

➲ Plants

Corner + plant = true love. Some corners in a room could be dark and perceived as boring. A big plant together with a lamp is always a winning concept.

Avoid:

» giving the TV the best wall
» having a picture above the sofa which is too large
» having a shelf on the wall above the sofa

Good to:

» place the sofa in power position
» create contrasts, for example a round carpet under a square table or vice versa
» have a soft pink throw to bring out when you need it (pink is healing and comforting)
» hide cables and electric devices as much as possible

Children's Rooms

Children's rooms are special because children are supposed to sleep and play in the same room. Because of that, their room should provide peace and quiet as well as inspiration for play.

Organisation and Storage

In this room, a very clear structure is needed. Every item should have its own place. It's good if toys 'live' somewhere - in a box, on a shelf and so on. Put boxes and books with the darker colours at the bottom and the lighter colours higher up. Put pictures on the boxes to make it clear what belongs where. Computers, tablets and TVs in the children's room emit radiation and everything that moves or makes a sound is a distraction. Children today often have an incredible amount of toys. Help them to choose toys and guide their play by not having everything out at the same time. You can put away some toys for a while and then bring them out again later to keep a feeling of novelty.

Safety

Children have an even bigger need for safety than adults, so take extra care to find a good power position for the bed. Children's room are often small so you might have to compromise to find the best solution. For example, you might have to place the foot of the bed under a window, but this doesn't matter as curtains or blinds drawn at night will slow down the flow of energy and calm the room. It's also important that the children's bed has a headboard and, if possible, a footboard.

Many children have a period when they love to build play houses to feel snug. A simple textile canopy above the bed will recreate this cosy safe feeling.

A bunk bed, if you are an adult, can feel claustrophobic and limiting. Most people find it more comfortable to sleep free from oppressive energy from the bunk above. For people sleeping in the upper bed, the ceiling can also oppress. Children, however, usually find it cosy to sleep in a bunk bed. The lower bed is immediately turned into a den.

As an adult, you usually want to avoid sleeping under a sloped ceiling since it gives a downward pressure which can disturb your sleep. But children, on the other hand, can find this a cosy part of the play house. It's important to listen to the children's needs. If they want to put the bed in a way which might seem odd to you, just let them. As they grow older, they will naturally change the position of the bed as they feel more secure.

Other furniture which needs to be in the power position is the desk, play table and reading chair. If children want company, then they will probably end up in the kitchen anyway.

Colours, shapes and materials in children's rooms

Too many different colours make the energy of the room busy. Therefore it's good to have a neutral colour on the walls. The room will probably be quite colourful with toys, rugs and storage boxes. Light colours make the room appear bigger. If the floor is a shade of brown the energy will be grounded and the children calmer.

To create balance between the five elements in a child's room, it's important to remember that everything in the room belongs to one of the five elements when it comes to colour, shape and material.

Can children be exposed to more colour than adults? It's easy to think so, when we decorate and paint for children. But that can create a colour overdose which leads to overstimulation and hyperactivity. The small ones are affected in the same way as adults, and also need peace and quiet from time to time.

After a week at school or kindergarten balance between yin and yang could be a walk in the woods, a picnic by the sea, or a cosy time together on the sofa.

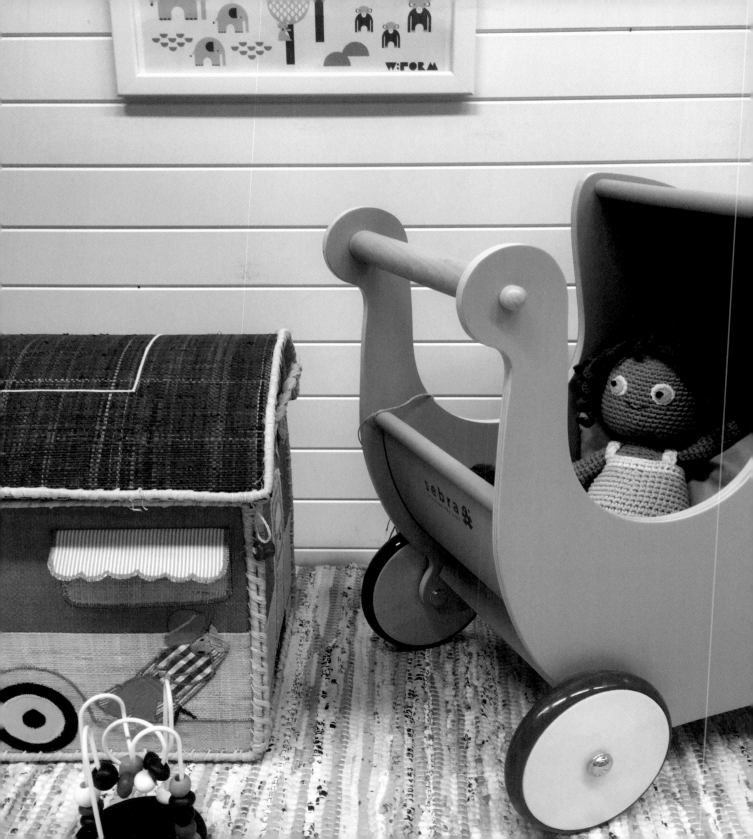

"Too many different colours create busy energy."

➲ Pictures and symbols

Everything in the room has a symbolic meaning which is interpreted by your subconscious mind. Therefore it's good to use symbols which provide security and happiness. It could be something which the children appreciate and love, for example a poster showing Paddington or Pippi Longstocking. It could also be pictures of your own child playing, painting or dancing. A loving picture of the family could also be great.

➲ Energy enhancers

In a children's room, energy enhancers are rarely needed. Often there are just too many things, colours and shapes which activate and raise the energy in the room. Removing some of these objects calms the room down. Plants, which are generally energy enhancers, are still good to add as they freshen the room. Plants with small soft leaves could be one way of getting more yin and calmness into the room, while also providing the wood element. Choose plants you know are toxin-free and not prickly.

➲ Tips for sleeping

A good night's sleep for the children is important. Create 'yin time': slow down one hour before bed-time. Turn off the TV, play calm and relaxing music or sounds from nature. Turn down the light, light a candle, and create a harmonious moment. Make teeth brushing fun. Read a book together, as the closeness and love makes children feel secure. Going to bed will be easier, and it will feel better both for the parents and the child. Also remember to pull the curtains or blinds to make the room calm and better for sleep.

Things that can disturb children's sleep:

» sleeping on Curry lines*

» a big and heavy lampshade above the bed

» a hard headboard

» a reading lamp above the head

» a shelf on the wall above the bed

» a big and heavy picture on the wall above the bed

» computers and tablets

» TV and mobile phones

» pictures which create disturbing emotions

» too much colour

» clutter

» toys in the bed

» sharp corners pointing towards the bed

» being unable to see the door from the bed

*Curry lines are energy lines (geopathic stress) that can give you both bad sleep and bad health.

Bathroom

The bathroom is a room with great demands placed upon it. It should work well for a quick shower in the morning as well as for a relaxing bath in the evening. If you have children, you probably want it to be big and spacious. The bathroom should also be a room where you can relax and be yourself without being disturbed by others.

Clean and fresh = good energy

The bathroom is about cleansing and renewal. This is the place where we leave the old behind to come out alert and fresh. The bathroom is inevitably connected withdrains and sewers, things we don't want to get close to. You can avoid bad energy by having the toilet lid and bathroom door closed whenever possible.

Wood and earth element - important in the bathroom

To keep the freshness, it's important to keep the bathroom clean and tidy. Fresh and healthy plants help to keep a good feeling in the bathroom. They belong to the wood element and have an uplifting energy that reverse the sewer's downward pull.

However, bathrooms are often dark and windowless which makes it difficult for plants to survive. In this situation you can still introduce the wood element with artificial plants, green-coloured towels, a green bathmat or other green details. Green belongs to the wood element and, like your bathroom, represents cleansing and renewal. If you like artificial plants, it's completely OK according to feng shui, as there are many well-made high-quality ones. In our opinion, an artificial plant is better than having no wood element at all.

To introduce the earth element, you could put some round brown pebbles around the plughole in the sink or bathtub. The pebbles hold back the bad energy from the sewer while the brown (earth element) creates a warm and dry feeling in the humid bathroom. Storage made of natural wood or rattan is often better than plastic and a good way of bringing in the earth element.

Even if you have a new and stylish bathroom, the sewer energies are still there. That's why you want to avoid putting bathroom and bedroom together. The bedroom and bathroom have completely different energies that don't mingle well with each other. It's better to keep these room separated, and ideally not even next door to each other.

Feeling safe

The fact that you are naked in the bathroom makes you extra vulnerable so make this room soft and cosy. Minimise sharp edges and corners or prickly plants. Mirrors with corners and no frame can give a hard and uncomfortable feeling. It's easy to fix by just putting a frame around it. A round mirror has a gentle shape and does not need a frame. Also think about how your bathtub is placed (power position). Since you are often semi-clad or naked it's important that you also feel safe around the window. A frosted window, window plastic or curtain will help you feel secure.

➲ Clearing the clutter

Clearing the clutter is a good way of bringing good energy into the bathroom. Don't have too many bottles or products out at the same time. Instead, have one good shampoo, conditioner and soap. Finish everything in the bottles before buying new ones.

➲ Scent

This is the room where we want to hide unpleasant smells. Maybe there is an attractive scent from your soaps and toiletries, otherwise you can use a fragranced candle or something else which brings out a lovely scent.

➲ Lighting

As in all other rooms, it's important to have many different kinds of lighting for different activities. You can aim bright spotlights at the mirror but have softer lighting when you relax in a nice hot bath in the evening. Candles are always good for creating ambience and increasing energy.

Remember:
- » towels in the same colour give a feeling of calmness - yin
- » towels in different colours give a feeling of activity - yang
- » closed storage cupboards make the room calmer

Challenges in the bathroom:
- » a small and dark room
- » damp, which can lead to mould
- » blocked drains

Avoid:
- » sitting with the door behind you when you are in the bath
- » having a large lamp or hanging plant above the bath tub

Ideally:
- » the toilet is located so you feel safe - not too far away from the door
- » the bathroom should have good ventilation
- » the door is closed and the toilet lid is down
- » all mirrors are undamaged and clean

Thanks

Thanks to you who read this book.

Jenny:
To my grandmother Astrid. Before you passed, you said 'write your books, fulfil your dreams'. So, grandma, I did it, thinking of you.

My family: Jenny Wahlberg, our children Georg and Marley, my mother Kerstin Johnsson, my father Rolf Söderström and my sister Julia Jonsson. Susanna Utbult, my teacher, colleague and friend.

Susanna:
Thanks to my family - I love you. Thanks, Jenny, for your friendship and the good laughs. A special thank you to Maria Lacik and Jessica Nyström for great teamwork.

MARIA LACIK – photographs – Instagram: homesinharmony
(pages 5, 12, 15, 20, 23, 27 ,37, 39, 40, 43, 46, 49, 50, 52, 69, 71, 72, 76, 87 and 91)

JESSICA VESTERLUND NYSTRÖM – layout

ALICE DANIELSSON – illustrations (pages 29 and 34)

MARIA LAVRELL – photograph (page 8)

SWEEF – www.sweef.se

FARMHOUSE FRIENDS – www.farmhouseshop.se

FAT CAT – www.fatcatstockholm.se

MERALEVA – www.meraleva.com

HOUSE & FLOWERS – www.houseandflowers.se

LILLING COTTAGE – www.lilling.se

For more inspiration about feng shui, follow us on

Instagram:
nordicfengshui and inviteflow

Facebook:
Nordic School of Feng Shui
and Invite flow

You are welcome to contact us at:
susanna@nordic-fengshui.com

jenny@inviteflow.com